THE NEW JERSEY DEVILS

BY

MARK STEWART

Content Consultant
Denis Gibbons
Society for International Hockey Research

NORWOOD HOUSE PRESS

CHICAGO, ILLINOIS

Norwood House Press
P.O. Box 316598
Chicago, Illinois 60631

For information regarding Norwood House Press, please visit our website at:
www.norwoodhousepress.com or call 866-565-2900.

PHOTO CREDITS:
All photos courtesy Getty Images except the following:
Topps, Inc. (6, 14, 21, 37, 40 top & bottom left, 41, 43), New Jersey Devils (7),
National Hockey League (9, 41 left), Associated Press (18, 32, 38),
O-Pee-Chee Ltd. (23), Kansas City Scouts (34),
Author's Collection (35 top left, 41 bottom left).
Cover photo: Jim McIsaac/Getty Images
Special thanks to Topps, Inc.

Editor: Mike Kennedy
Designer: Ron Jaffe
Project Management: Black Book Partners, LLC.
Research: Joshua Zaffos
Special thanks to John Fontana and Marc & Bruce Lowe

LIBRARY OF CONGRESS CATALOGING-IN-PUBLICATION DATA

Stewart, Mark, 1960-
  The New Jersey Devils / by Mark Stewart.
      p. cm. -- (Team spirit)
  Includes bibliographical references and index.
  Summary: "Presents the history and accomplishments of the New Jersey
Devils hockey team. Includes highlights of players, coaches, and awards,
quotes, timeline, maps, glossary, and website"--Provided by publisher.
  ISBN-13: 978-1-59953-402-2 (library edition : alk. paper)
  ISBN-10: 1-59953-402-9 (library edition : alk. paper)
  1. New Jersey Devils (Hockey team)--History--Juvenile literature. I.
Title.
  GV848.N38S74 2011
  796.962'640974932--dc22
                                              2010011621

Manufactured in the United States of America in North Mankato, Minnesota.
159N—072010

COVER PHOTO: The Devils celebrate a goal during the 2008–09 season.

Table of Contents

SPORTS WORDS & VOCABULARY WORDS: In this book, you will find many words that are new to you. You may also see familiar words used in new ways. The glossary on page 46 gives the meanings of hockey words, as well as "everyday" words that have special hockey meanings. These words appear in **bold type** throughout the book. The glossary on page 47 gives the meanings of vocabulary words that are not related to hockey. They appear in ***bold italic type*** throughout the book.

Meet the Devils

There is a legend in New Jersey of a fast-moving monster that swoops in on its victims in the dead of night. Most people know this creature as the Jersey Devil. Scientists say it does not exist. New Jersey hockey fans would disagree. They have been rooting for the Devils since the 1980s.

The Devils win with hard checking, sharp passing, and smart defense. New Jersey looks for players who can outskate and outlast their opponents. From there, teamwork takes over—no team plays better than the Devils when they play as one. They wait patiently for other teams to make risky passes. That is when the Devils live up to their name and move in for the kill.

This book tells the story of the Devils. After years of struggling, they discovered the key to championship hockey. Along the way, the team made stops in two other cities. But once the Devils arrived in New Jersey, they finally felt right at home.

John Madden and Colin White congratulate Martin Brodeur after a victory during the 2008–09 season.

Way Back When

Starting in the 1960s, towns across North America were gripped by "hockey fever." Fans everywhere, it seemed, wanted a **professional** team. Soon, the **National Hockey League (NHL)** and **World Hockey Association (WHA)** were in a mad race to move into new cities. For the 1974–75 season, the NHL put teams in Kansas City, Missouri and Washington, D.C. The Kansas City Scouts would one day become the Devils.

SCOUTS

RIGHT WING

WILF PAIEMENT

Before moving east to New Jersey, the team actually moved west to Colorado. The Scouts were not drawing many fans, so the owners sold the club to a group in Denver, Colorado. The new owners renamed the team the Rockies. It was the first time in more than 40 years that an NHL team switched cities.

The Rockies had some good players, including Wilf Paiement, Barry Beck, Lanny McDonald, and Chico Resch. But winning did not come easily. The Rockies tried to draw fans with the promise of rough play. But the

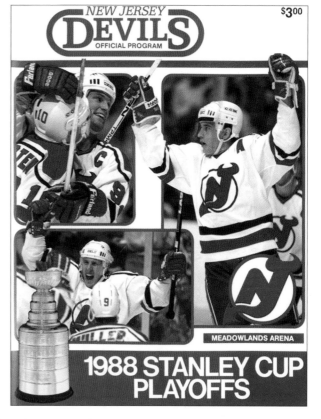

league wanted its teams to focus on exciting skaters, not bruising fighters.

In 1982, a businessman named John McMullen bought the Rockies and moved the team to his home state of New Jersey. The club was renamed the Devils. New Jersey rebuilt around talented young players, including Kirk Muller, John MacLean, Pat Verbeek, Brendan Shanahan, Bruce Driver, and Sean Burke. In 1987–88, the Devils made the **playoffs** for the first time, and then nearly reached the **Stanley Cup Finals.**

Over the next 15 seasons, the Devils won the **Stanley Cup** three times. They were champions of the NHL in 1995, 2000, and 2003. The key to their success was a defensive style that slowed down opponents at center ice before they could organize their offensive attack. The Devils would wait patiently for the other team to become frustrated and make a mistake. Then they would steal the puck and score!

New Jersey did not stock its **roster** with superstars. Instead, the Devils found tough, hardworking skaters who understood the

importance of playing as a team. The club's scoring leaders included forwards Claude Lemieux, Patrik Elias, Bobby Holik, Jason Arnott, Petr Sykora, and Scott Gomez. The defense was led by Scott Stevens, Scott Niedermayer, Brian Rafalski, and Ken Daneyko.

Because New Jersey concentrated on defense, many of the team's victories came in very close games. Often the difference was

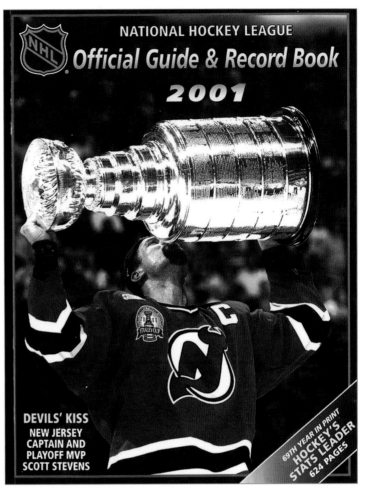

NATIONAL HOCKEY LEAGUE
Official Guide & Record Book
2001

DEVILS' KISS
NEW JERSEY CAPTAIN AND PLAYOFF MVP SCOTT STEVENS

69TH YEAR IN PRINT
HOCKEY'S STATS LEADER
624 PAGES

goaltending. This was where the Devils were strongest. Goalie Martin Brodeur was "between the pipes" for all three Stanley Cup championships. The bigger the game, the better he played. Brodeur would go on to break almost every NHL goaltending record. He would become the most famous player in team history and lead the Devils through the first *decade* of the 21st *century*.

LEFT: Martin Brodeur turns away a shot.   **ABOVE**: The NHL's 2001 *Official Guide & Record Book* shows Scott Stevens kissing the Stanley Cup.

The Team Today

The only thing harder than winning a Stanley Cup is following up with another championship. The Devils showed they could do this by capturing the Cup three times in nine seasons. With each title, they learned a little more about what it takes to be the best. At the same time, other NHL clubs learned more about the Devils' style of play.

To keep improving, New Jersey built around a group of **veterans** from the 2003 Stanley Cup team. Martin Brodeur, Patrik Elias, Jamie Langenbrunner, Colin White, and Jay Pandolfo set the example for their new teammates. Stars such as Zach Parise, Ilya Kovalchuk, and Travis Zajac knew exactly what was expected of them when they joined the team.

The names and faces in the New Jersey **lineup** change from season to season, but one thing stays the same. The Devils will never be a team of superstars. Instead they try to be a super team. That has been their winning *strategy* every time they have held the Stanley Cup high.

Travis Zajac, Ilya Kovalchuk, and Zach Parise can't contain their excitement after a goal in a 2009–10 game.

Home Ice

For most of their history, the Devils shared their arena with the New Jersey Nets basketball team. It was part of the Meadowlands Sports Complex. The stadium of the New York Giants and Jets football teams was also located there.

The Devils moved to a beautiful new home for the 2007–08 season. Devils fans like to call it "The Rock." The Devils' arena is located in downtown Newark. It has several high-definition (HD) video screens and scoreboards. It also has a mural that celebrates great moments in New Jersey sports. Martin Brodeur, Scott Stevens, and Ken Daneyko are among the athletes pictured.

BY THE NUMBERS

- *The team's arena has 17,625 seats for hockey.*
- *There are 76 luxury suites in the arena.*
- *As of 2009–10, the Devils have retired two numbers—3 (Ken Daneyko) and 4 (Scott Stevens).*

The Devils battle for the puck during a 2008–09 game at their arena.

Dressed for Success

When the team played in Kansas City and Colorado, its main uniform color was blue. The Scouts *logo* showed a Native American on a horse. The Rockies logo was a mountain surrounding the letter *C*.

After their move to New Jersey, the Devils switched their main colors to red and green. Their new logo had an *N* and *J* with a devil's horns and tail. In 1992–93, the team started using black instead of green. Today, the players usually wear red sweaters at home and white sweaters on the road.

Before the Devils ever played a game, some fans complained that the team was named after an evil being. The club met with religious leaders to make sure the name would not be a problem. Everyone agreed that the meaning of "devil" was clear—it was a make-believe monster and nothing more.

Barry Beck models the Colorado uniform. The team logo is in the upper left-hand corner of the card.

UNIFORM BASICS

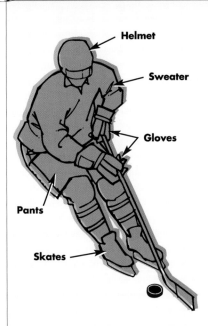

Helmet

Sweater

Gloves

Pants

Skates

The hockey uniform has five important parts:
- Helmet • Sweater • Pants
- Gloves • Skates

Hockey helmets are made of hard plastic with softer padding inside. Some players also wear visors to protect their eyes.

The hockey uniform top is called a sweater. Players wear padding underneath it to protect their shoulders, spine and ribs. Padded hockey pants, or "breezers," extend from the waist to the knees. Players also wear padding on their knees and shins.

Hockey gloves protect the top of the hand and the wrist. Only a thin layer of leather covers the palm, which helps a player control his stick. A goalie wears two different gloves—one for catching pucks and one for blocking them. Goalies also wear heavy leg pads and a mask. They paint their masks to match their personalities and team colors.

All players wear hockey skates. The blade is curved at each end. The skate top is made from metal, plastic, nylon, and either real or *synthetic* leather. Goalies wear skates that have extra protection on the toe and ankle.

Patrik Elias wears the team's 2009–10 home uniform.

We Won!

During their first five years in New Jersey, the Devils did not have a single winning season. That changed in 1987–88, when they went 38–36–6 and made the playoffs for the first time. It took a goal in **overtime** by John MacLean in the final game of the regular season to grab the last playoff spot in the **Eastern Conference**.

In two exciting series, the Devils beat the New York Islanders and the Washington Capitals to reach the **Eastern Conference Finals**. New Jersey finally met its match in the Boston Bruins, who took the series in seven games. From that day forward, Devils fans would not settle for anything less than a trip to the Stanley Cup Finals.

They got their wish seven years later, when coach Jacques Lemaire made important changes to the club. Lemaire taught his players a defensive system called the **neutral zone trap**. This surprised many people—as a player, Lemaire was mostly known for his offensive skills. Meanwhile, he used four lines of forwards instead of three to keep his players from tiring out.

The Devils made the playoffs in 1994–95, but no one expected much of them. To win the Stanley Cup, a team must play well away from home. The Devils had won only eight games on the road that season. But once the playoffs started, they were sensational. The

Claude Lemieux holds the Stanley Cup in one arm and the Conn Smythe Trophy in the other.

Devils lost only once as the visiting team in their run to the Stanley Cup Finals. Even so, most fans expected the Detroit Red Wings to wipe them out.

"I'll never forget," says forward Randy McKay. "Four of the five papers were picking us to lose four straight. The other picked us to lose in three straight—they said we'd be so *embarrassed* after three that we wouldn't show up for four!"

Just the opposite happened. The Devils swept Detroit in four games. Everyone in the lineup chipped in. Neal Broten, who wasn't even on the team when the season started, scored the winning goals in Game 3 and Game 4. Claude Lemieux earned the Conn Smythe Trophy as the **Most Valuable Player (MVP)** of the playoffs. He scored 13 goals during the **postseason**.

The Devils won their second Stanley Cup in 1999–2000. Again, the experts expected little from the team. With eight games left in the regular season, New Jersey replaced coach Robbie Ftorek with Larry Robinson. Normally, this is not a good sign. But the players stuck together and beat three good teams to reach the finals. There they faced the Dallas Stars, who had won the Stanley Cup the year before.

Scott Stevens and Martin Brodeur starred for the Devils. The last two games against Dallas were thrilling. The Stars won Game 5 in triple-overtime. The Devils bounced back two nights later to win in double-overtime. Jason Arnott scored the game-winning goal.

New Jersey's third Stanley Cup came three years later. This time, expectations were very high. But the Anaheim Ducks put up a great fight in the Stanley Cup Finals. New Jersey needed seven games to

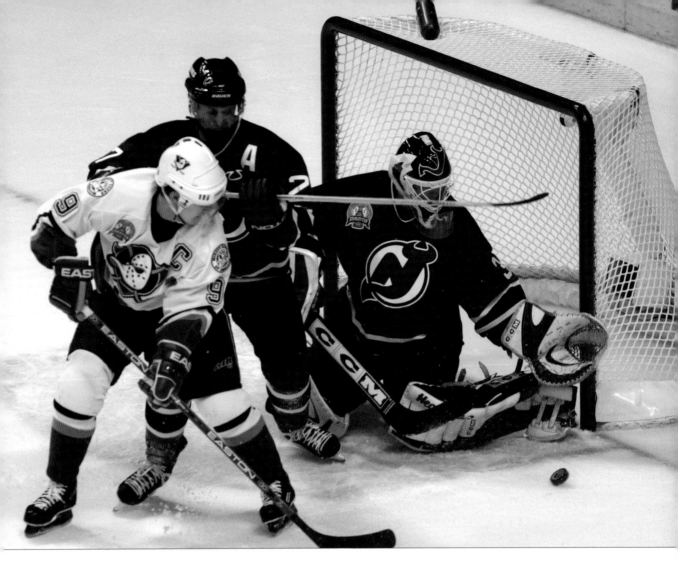

beat Anaheim. Brodeur recorded three **shutouts**, while Stevens and Scott Niedermayer played brilliant defense. As usual, everyone on the team contributed, including left wing Jeff Friesen, who scored five goals in the finals. Before that season, Friesen had been a member of the Ducks!

LEFT: Jason Arnott leaps into the arms of Scott Stevens after scoring the goal that won the 2000 Stanley Cup.
ABOVE: Martin Brodeur makes a save against the Anaheim Ducks as Scott Niedermayer keeps an opponent away.

Go-To Guys

To be a true star in the NHL, you need more than a great slapshot. You have to be a "go-to guy"—someone teammates trust to make the winning play when the seconds are ticking away in a big game. Fans of the Scouts, Rockies, and Devils have had a lot to cheer about over the years, including these great stars …

THE PIONEERS

WILF PAIEMENT   Right Wing

• BORN: 10/16/1955 • PLAYED FOR TEAM: 1974–75 TO 1979–80

Wilf Paiement was the second pick in the 1974 NHL **draft**. He was a rough player with a hard, accurate shot. The result was a lot of goals—and a lot of time in the penalty box!

JOHN MACLEAN   Right Wing

• BORN: 11/20/1964 • PLAYED FOR TEAM: 1983–84 TO 1997–98

John MacLean scored more than 40 goals three seasons in a row for New Jersey. MacLean was known as a **clutch** player. His overtime goal at the end of the 1987–88 season sent the Devils to the playoffs for the first time.

KEN DANEYKO   Defenseman

• BORN: 4/17/1964 • PLAYED FOR TEAM: 1983–84 TO 2002–03

Ken Daneyko was a "stay-at-home" defenseman. He was always in position to protect his net and didn't fire many shots against the opposing goalie. Daneyko spent all 20 of his NHL seasons with the Devils.

KIRK MULLER   Left Wing/Center

• BORN: 2/8/1966   • PLAYED FOR TEAM: 1984–85 TO 1990–91

The heart of the Devils during the 1980s was Kirk Muller. He played hard at both ends of the ice. In 1987–88, Muller led New Jersey to within one game of the Stanley Cup Finals.

Kirk Muller

CLAUDE LEMIEUX   Right Wing

• BORN: 7/16/1965

• PLAYED FOR TEAM: 1990–91 TO 1994–95 & 1999–00

When the playoffs started, Claude Lemieux went from being a good player to a great one. Lemieux was an excellent leader who had a knack for scoring big goals. He helped the Devils win two Stanley Cups.

SCOTT STEVENS   Defenseman

• BORN: 4/1/1964 • PLAYED FOR TEAM: 1991–92 TO 2003–04

Scott Stevens was a human wrecking ball. He used his size and speed to deliver crunching checks. Most of all, Stevens was a winner. When he retired, he had played in more regular-season victories (879) than any player in history.

MARTIN BRODEUR   Goalie

• Born: 5/6/1972   • First Season with Team: 1991–92

Few goalies have been as good for as long as Martin Brodeur. He was the youngest netminder to reach 500 victories. Brodeur also set NHL career marks for wins, shutouts, and games played by a goalie.

SCOTT NIEDERMAYER   Defenseman

• Born: 8/31/1973   • Played for Team: 1991–92 to 2003–04

Scott Niedermayer played great defense and was a leader on the **power play** for the Devils. In 2003–04, the team allowed just two goals per game. After the season, Niedermayer won the Norris Trophy as the NHL's top defenseman.

BOBBY HOLIK   Center

• Born: 1/1/1971

• Played for Team: 1992–93 to 2001–02 & 2008–09

Bobby Holik always demanded the best from himself and his teammates. No one on the team played harder or wanted to win more. Holik was a good scorer who never backed down from an opponent.

ABOVE: Bobby Holik
RIGHT: Zach Parise

PATRIK ELIAS   Left Wing

• BORN: 4/13/1976   • FIRST SEASON WITH TEAM: 1995–96

Most scorers have a favorite spot to shoot from. Patrik Elias could fire the puck from anywhere on the ice and find the back of the net. He scored his 300th goal as a Devil in 2009–10.

SCOTT GOMEZ   Center

• BORN: 12/23/1979   • PLAYED FOR TEAM: 1999–00 TO 2006–07

Scott Gomez was the NHL's first Latino player. He was an *agile* and clever skater who could thread passes through the smallest openings. Gomez led the Devils with 51 **assists** as a **rookie**.

ZACH PARISE   Left Wing

• BORN: 7/28/84

• FIRST SEASON WITH TEAM: 2005–06

Zach Parise learned to play hockey from his father J.P., who played in the NHL **All-Star Game** twice. Parise turned out to be a good student. In 2009–10, he led the team in points (goals plus assists) for the third straight season.

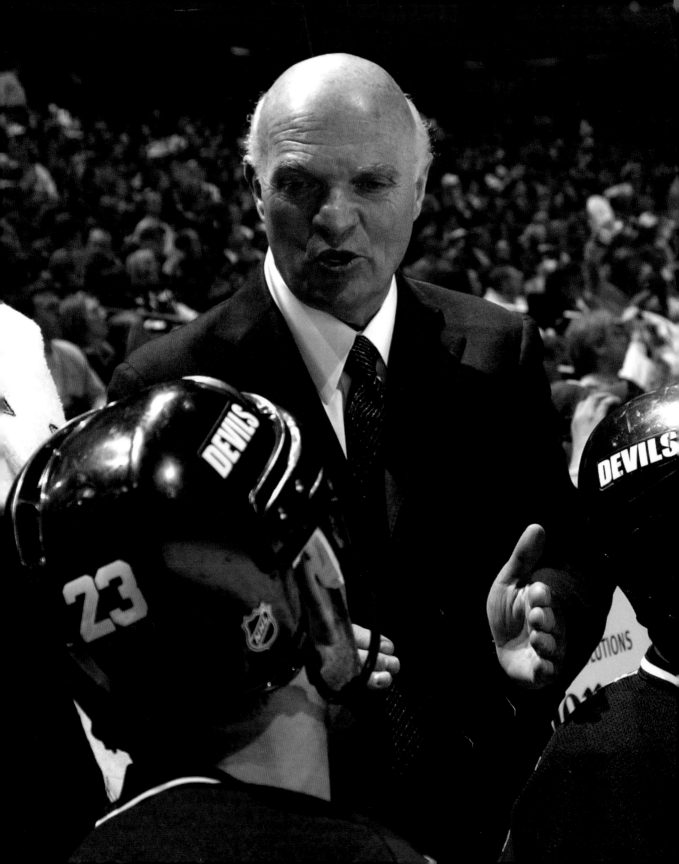

Behind the Bench

The Devils give their coaches a lot of power, and they expect great results. That is the biggest reason why the team has made so many coaching changes over the years. If the Devils are not reaching their *potential,* the coach—not the players—takes the blame. Starting in 1987, the person deciding who should coach the Devils was Lou Lamoriello. When Lamoriello took control of the team, he had no experience in the NHL. Lamoriello knew college hockey inside-out, though. So he knew how to *assemble* and run a hockey team. The Devils became winners almost every year under Lamoriello.

New Jersey always tries to find a coach whose style matches the players on the roster. Jim Schoenfeld, Robbie Ftorek, Pat Burns, Larry Robinson, and Jacques Lemaire all had different approaches to the game. When Lamoriello could not find the leader he wanted, he coached the team himself.

What all New Jersey coaches have in common is a focus on **team chemistry**. Whether they are on the attack or defending their own net, the Devils are at their best when they work together. The results speak for themselves.

Lou Lamoriello discusses strategy with Scott Gomez during a 2006–07 game.

One Great Day

Many fans believe that New Jersey's greatest moment came a few minutes after *losing* a third straight playoff game to the Philadelphia Flyers in the spring of 2000. The Devils walked off the ice knowing they had dug themselves a deep hole. They were now behind three games to one in the Eastern Conference Finals. No team had ever won the conference finals after losing three games in a row.

Larry Robinson had been named coach of the Devils with only eight games left in the season. The players were still learning his style. Up until this day, they knew him to be a serious, quiet man. It turned out they didn't know him at all. Robinson came into the dressing room with fire in his eyes after the loss to the Flyers.

"You guys tried it your way for a while," he screamed. "Now I'm telling you what to do and you'll do it!"

Robinson told the Devils that they had been playing selfish hockey. Each player was trying to be a hero, instead of playing together as a team. He mentioned two players by name, Scott Stevens

Larry Robinson and Ken Daneyko share a laugh in March of 2007.

and Ken Daneyko. Of all the Devils, they had been playing the best. Their teammates were **stunned**.

"Individuals win awards—teams win championships," Robinson explained. "We can be the first team to make history. No other team has come back from three-to-one. It's a challenge we should accept."

Robinson was exactly right. The Devils began playing together on offense and defense. The Flyers did not know how to respond. New Jersey won the next three games. From there, the Devils were unstoppable. In the Stanley Cup Finals, they beat the Dallas Stars in six games to win the championship.

Legend Has It

Who was the most nervous person during the 2002–03 Stanley Cup Finals?

LEGEND HAS IT that Carol Niedermayer was. One son, Scott, played for the Devils. Another, Rob, played for the Anaheim Ducks. So many reporters tried to interview her that the Devils had to set up

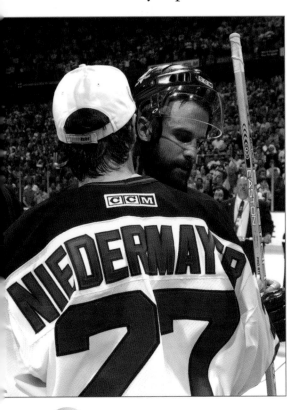

a *press conference*. Carol admitted that she was rooting for the Ducks. Scott had already won two championships with the Devils, so it would be nice for Rob to get one. Both of her sons played well, but the Devils *prevailed*. Four years later, the Niedermayer brothers made things easier on their mom. Scott had joined Anaheim. He and Rob were on the ice together when the Ducks won the Stanley Cup in 2006–07.

Scott and Rob Niedermayer hug after the 2002–03 Stanley Cup Finals.

Was the team originally named after a hairstyle?

LEGEND HAS IT that the Scouts were … well, sort of. When the NHL agreed to start a team in Kansas City, the owners looked for a clever way to include the states of Missouri and Kansas in the name. They chose Mohawks. *MO* is the **abbreviation** for Missouri. *Hawks* is short for Jayhawks, the nickname of the most popular college basketball team in Kansas. A "mohawk" is also the name of a wild hairstyle. When the Chicago Blackhawks heard about this plan, they complained to the league—Mohawks was very similar to Blackhawks. The owners changed the team name to Scouts, after the famous statue of an Indian scout that overlooks Kansas City.

Which Devil was hockey's all-time best bargain?

LEGEND HAS IT that Martin Brodeur was. During the 1994–95 season, Brodeur was the lowest-paid full-time player in the league. The Devils sure got their money's worth. Brodeur led the Devils to the Stanley Cup. In 1995–96, he got a well-deserved raise of more than 10 times his previous salary.

It Really Happened

Devils fans often argue about the biggest "stop" in team history. Mostly, they talk about Martin Brodeur, who has made hundreds of great saves. But more than a few Devils will tell you that the man who made the most important stop wasn't wearing a New Jersey sweater. He was wearing a bus driver's uniform.

Toward the end of the 2002–03 season, the Devils traded for Grant Marshall. He was so new that one day the team bus left for the game without him—and no one noticed! This wasn't just any game. It was the last game in New Jersey's playoff series with the Tampa Bay Lightning.

When Marshall saw the bus roaring away, he grabbed his bags and ran after it. He chased it up a hill and down a street before the driver spotted him in the mirror and stopped to let him on. That night, the Devils and Lightning played three overtime periods.

As the game wore on, Marshall wondered what it would be like to score the winning goal. He pictured himself at the bottom of a pile of happy teammates. "I was really hoping to get the puck and get the goal for the guys," he remembers, "and have them cheering and going crazy."

The Devils scream with joy after Grant Marshall's overtime goal.

In the third overtime, Marshall saw his chance. The Devils set up a play for Scott Niedermayer to blast a slapshot at the Lightning goal. Marshall skated in front of the net to block the goalie's view.

The goalie stopped the puck, but it dribbled right onto Marshall's stick. He whacked a backhand into the net to win the game and the series. With help from their newest teammate, the Devils went on to win the Stanley Cup.

Team Spirit

When a team wins the Stanley Cup, a big parade usually follows. The players ride in cars or on floats through the middle of the city. The fans cheer them from the sidewalks. When the Devils have won the Stanley Cup, this wasn't possible. They played in an arena that was located in the middle of a swamp. They did not "belong" to any one city.

The team's solution was to drive around the parking lot of their arena. It sounded like a strange idea, but it turned out to be a great one. Fans got there early and started their own tailgating parties. The players were able to spend time with the fans instead of simply driving by them. Many ended up tailgating themselves. Everyone had fun.

Now the Devils play in a new arena—The Rock, in the city of Newark. Their next victory celebration probably will go down Broad Street and Market Street, two of the city's major roads. The fans will stand and cheer. But they will never forget those first "parking lot parades."

The Devils pose for a team picture during their "parking lot parade" after the team's third Stanley Cup.

33

Timeline

The hockey season is played from October through June. That means each season takes place at the end of one year and the beginning of the next. In this timeline, the accomplishments of the Scouts, Rockies, and Devils are shown by season.

1976–77
The Scouts move to Colorado and become the Rockies.

1983–84
New Jersey hosts the All-Star Game.

1974–75
The team joins the NHL as the Kansas City Scouts.

1982–83
The Devils play their first season in New Jersey.

1987–88
The Devils have their first winning season.

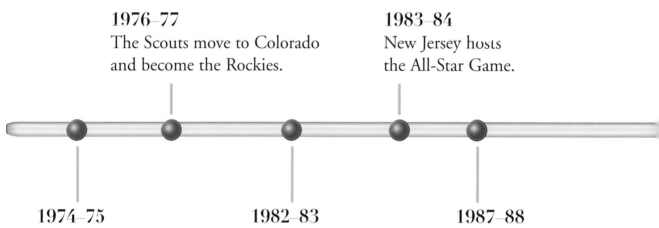

A team photo from the Scouts' first season.

A sticker from the team's early years.

Coach Pat Burns lifts the Stanley Cup in 2003.

1994–95
Claude Lemieux leads the Devils to their first Stanley Cup.

2002–03
The team wins its third Stanley Cup.

1999–00
The Devils win their second championship.

2003–04
Scott Niedermayer wins the Norris Trophy.

2009–10
Martin Brodeur sets an NHL record with his 104th shutout.

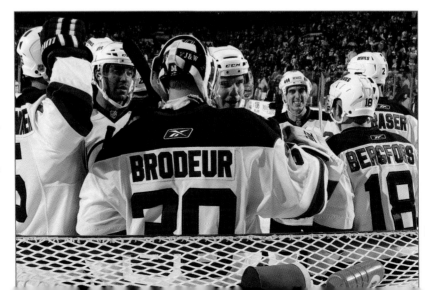

Teammates congratulate Martin Brodeur after his record-setting shutout.

Fun Facts

FINAL TOUCH

During the 1999–2000 season, Martin Brodeur became the first goalie to "score" a game-winning goal. With the score tied 2–2, the Philadelphia Flyers shot the puck into their own net by mistake. Since Brodeur was the last Devil to touch the puck, he got credit for the goal.

LITTLE BIG MAN

At 5′ 7″ tall, Brian Gionta was one of the smallest players in team history. Even so, he put up one of the Devils' biggest numbers— a team-record 48 goals in 2005–06.

DREAM SEASON

The 2002–03 season was like a dream for rookie Mike Rupp. In the first game of his career, he scored two goals. In the final game of the season, he scored the goal that won the Stanley Cup for the Devils.

FOREIGN EXCHANGE

The Devils have had some of the Czech Republic's greatest players in their lineup, including Bobby Holik, Patrik Elias, and Petr Sykora. They have had several Russian stars, too, including Ilya Kovalchuk, Slava Fetisov, Alexander Mogilny, and Sergei Brylin.

LUCKY SEVEN

Most goalies would have been *ashamed* to allow six goals in their first NHL start. Not Sean Burke. New Jersey's 21-year-old rookie had a big smile on his face when the final siren sounded. His teammates had scored seven times for a 7–6 victory.

WORTH THE WAIT

The Devils hold the NHL record for going the longest without being awarded a **penalty shot**, 829 games. Their first didn't come until the 1984–85 season. Rocky Trottier scored against the Edmonton Oilers.

LEFT: Brian Gionta waves to the fans during the 2005–06 season.
ABOVE: Viacheslav "Slava" Fetisov

Talking Hockey

"After all those years of frustration, of not having good teams or not making the playoffs … we just looked at each other and said, 'We won the Stanley Cup!'"

—Bruce Driver, on the team's reaction when they won their first championship

"Playoffs are the best time of the year. That's what you play for. That's when hockey is fun. Everything's a challenge, every game means so much."

—Colin White, on the thrill of playing for the Stanley Cup

"I was demanding of myself and my teammates. I was willing to do whatever it took to win."

—Claude Lemieux, on how he approached the playoffs

"We were on such a fun run, we didn't want it to end."

—Kirk Muller, on the Devils' playoff success in 1987–88

"I don't score highlight reel goals. They come from work, from getting into the corners, getting a little dirty."

—*Zach Parise, on doing the "dirty work" on the ice*

"He became an instant legend as a coach. He was already a legend as a player."

—*Bobby Holik, on Larry Robinson, who was an NHL All-Star in his playing days*

"I loved the way he coached, the way he approached hockey, the way he treated his players."

—*Neal Broten, on Jacques Lemaire*

"You don't get famous by being a Devil. You get recognized for being part of a winning team."

—*Martin Brodeur, on being a hockey celebrity in New Jersey*

LEFT: Bruce Driver lifts the Stanley Cup.
ABOVE: Zach Parise

For the Record

The great Devils teams and players have left their marks on the record books. These are the "best of the best" ...

Martin Brodeur

Scott Gomez

DEVILS AWARD WINNERS

CALDER TROPHY
TOP ROOKIE

Martin Brodeur	1993–94
Scott Gomez	1999–00

CONN SMYTHE TROPHY
MVP DURING PLAYOFFS

Claude Lemieux	1994–95
Scott Stevens	1999–00

JAMES NORRIS MEMORIAL TROPHY
TOP DEFENSIVE PLAYER

Scott Niedermayer	2003–04

FRANK J. SELKE AWARD
BEST DEFENSIVE FORWARD

John Madden	2000–01

VEZINA TROPHY
TOP GOALTENDER

Martin Brodeur	2002–03
Martin Brodeur	2003–04
Martin Brodeur	2006–07
Martin Brodeur	2007–08

JACK ADAMS AWARD
COACH OF THE YEAR

Jacques Lemaire	1993–94

John Madden

DEVILS ACHIEVEMENTS

ACHIEVEMENT	YEAR
Stanley Cup Champions	1994–95
Stanley Cup Champions	1999–00
Stanley Cup Finalists	2000–01
Stanley Cup Champions	2002–03

TOP RIGHT: Patrik Elias, a hero for the 1999–00 and 2002–03 Stanley Cup champs.
BOTTOM RIGHT: A pin that Devils fans wore in the 1990s.
BELOW: Scott Stevens celebrates New Jersey's 1995 Stanley Cup.

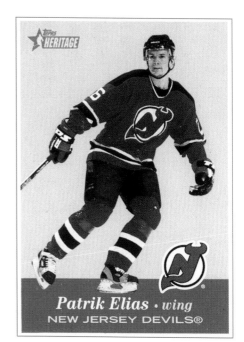

Patrik Elias • wing
NEW JERSEY DEVILS®

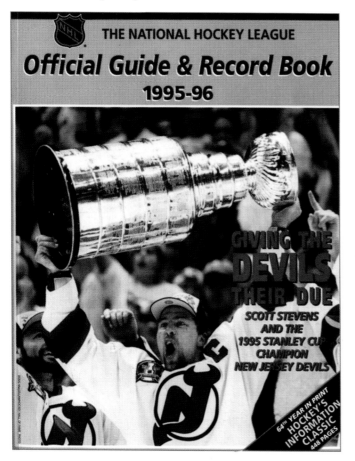

THE NATIONAL HOCKEY LEAGUE
Official Guide & Record Book
1995-96

GIVING THE DEVILS THEIR DUE
SCOTT STEVENS AND THE 1995 STANLEY CUP CHAMPION NEW JERSEY DEVILS

64TH YEAR IN PRINT
HOCKEY'S INFORMATION CLASSIC
448 PAGES

I ♥ THE DEVILS

Pinpoints

T he history of a hockey team is made up of many smaller stories. These stories take place all over the map—not just in the city a team calls "home." Match the pushpins on these maps to the Team Facts and you will begin to see the story of the Devils unfold!

TEAM FACTS

1 Newark, New Jersey—*The Devils have played here since 2007–08.*

2 Cloquet, Minnesota—*Jamie Langenbrunner was born here.*

3 Winchester, Massachusetts—*Jay Pandolfo was born here.*

4 Denver, Colorado—*The team moved here from Kansas City in 1976–77.*

5 Anchorage, Alaska—*Scott Gomez was born here.*

6 Montreal, Quebec, Canada—*Martin Brodeur was born here.*

7 Windsor, Ontario, Canada—*Ken Daneyko was born here.*

8 Moose Jaw, Saskatchewan, Canada—*Chico Resch was born here.*

9 Oshawa, Ontario, Canada—*John MacLean was born here.*

10 Vancouver, British Columbia, Canada—*Barry Beck was born here.*

11 Jihlava, Czechoslovakia*—*Bobby Holik was born here.*

12 Moscow, Russia—*Sergei Brylin was born here.*

* *Now known as the Czech Republic.*

John MacLean

43

Faceoff

Hockey is played between two teams of six skaters. Each team has a goalie, two defensemen, and a forward line that includes a left wing, right wing and center. The goalie's job is to stop the puck from crossing the red goal line. A hockey goal is six feet wide and four feet high. The hockey puck is a round disk made of hard rubber. It weighs approximately six ounces.

During a game, players skate as hard as they can for a full "shift." When they get tired, they take a seat on the bench, and a new group jumps off the bench and over the boards to take their place. Forwards play together in set groups, or "lines," and defensemen do too.

There are rules that prevent players from injuring or interfering with opponents. However, players are allowed to bump, or "check," each other when they battle for the puck. Because hockey is a fast game played by strong athletes, sometimes checks can be rough!

If a player breaks a rule, a penalty is called by the referee. For most penalties, the player must sit in the penalty box for two minutes. This gives the other team a one-skater advantage, or "power play." The team down a skater is said to be "short-handed."

NHL games have three 20-minute periods—60 minutes in all—and the team that scores the most goals when time has run out is the winner. If the score is tied, the teams play an overtime period. The first team to score during overtime wins. If the game is still tied, then it is decided

by a shootout—a one-on-one contest between the goalies and the best shooters. During the Stanley Cup playoffs, no shootouts are held. The teams play until the tie is broken.

Things happen so quickly in hockey that it is easy to overlook set plays. The next time you watch a game, see if you can spot these plays:

PLAY LIST

DEFLECTION—Sometimes a shooter does not try to score a goal. Instead, he aims his shot so that a teammate can touch the puck with his stick and suddenly change its direction. If the goalie is moving to stop the first shot, he may be unable to adjust to the "deflection."

GIVE-AND-GO—When a skater is closely guarded and cannot get an open shot, he sometimes passes to a teammate with the idea of getting a return pass in better position to shoot. The "give-and-go" works when the defender turns to follow the pass and loses track of his man. By the time he recovers, it is too late.

ONE-TIMER—When a player receives a pass, he must control the puck and position himself for a shot. This gives the defense a chance to react. Some players are skilled enough to shoot the instant a pass arrives for a "one-timer." A well-aimed one-timer is almost impossible to stop.

PULLING THE GOALIE—Sometimes in the final moments of a game, the team that is behind will try a risky play. To gain an extra skater, the team will pull the goalie out of the game and replace him with a center, wing, or defenseman. This gives the team a better chance to score. It also leaves the goal unprotected and allows the opponent to score an "empty-net goal."

Glossary

HOCKEY WORDS TO KNOW

ALL-STAR GAME—The annual game featuring the NHL's best players. Prior to 1967, the game was played at the beginning of the season between the league champion and an All-Star squad. Today it is played during the season. The game doesn't count in the standings.

ASSISTS—Passes that lead to a goal.

CLUTCH—Performing well under pressure.

DRAFT—The annual meeting during which NHL teams choose from a group of the best junior hockey, college, and international players. The draft is held each summer.

EASTERN CONFERENCE—A group of teams from the East. Each season, a team from the Eastern Conference faces a team from the Western Conference for the Stanley Cup.

EASTERN CONFERENCE FINALS—The series that determines which team from the East will face the best team from the West in the Stanley Cup Finals.

LINEUP—The list of players who are playing in a game.

MOST VALUABLE PLAYER (MVP)—The award given each year to the league's best player; also given to the best player in the playoffs and All-Star Game.

NATIONAL HOCKEY LEAGUE (NHL)—The league that began play in 1917–18 and is still in existence today.

NEUTRAL ZONE TRAP—A defensive style of play in which a team makes it difficult for the opponent to start an offensive attack. The neutral zone trap gives skaters little room to move and make passes.

OVERTIME—The extra 20-minute period played when a game is tied after 60 minutes. Teams continue playing overtime periods until one team scores a goal and wins.

PENALTY SHOT—A free shot at the opposing net and goalie awarded instead of a power play.

PLAYOFFS—The games played after the season to determine the league champion.

POSTSEASON—Another term for playoffs.

POWER PLAY—When one team has at least one extra player on the ice because of a penalty.

PROFESSIONAL—A player or team that plays a sport for money.

ROOKIE—A player in his first season.

ROSTER—The list of a team's active players.

SHUTOUTS—Games in which a team is prevented from scoring.

STANLEY CUP—The championship trophy of North American hockey since 1893, and of the NHL since 1927.

STANLEY CUP FINALS—The series that determines the NHL champion each season. It has been a best-of-seven series since 1939.

TEAM CHEMISTRY—The way players work together on and off the ice. Winning teams usually have good chemistry.

VETERANS—Players with great experience.

WORLD HOCKEY ASSOCIATION (WHA)—A rival league to the NHL that played from 1972–73 to 1978–79. When the WHA went out of business, four of its teams joined the NHL.

OTHER WORDS TO KNOW

ABBREVIATION—A shortened form of a word.

AGILE—Quick and graceful.

ASHAMED—Feeling guilty or disgraced.

ASSEMBLE—Put together.

CENTURY—A period of 100 years.

DECADE—A period of 10 years; also specific periods, such as the 1950s.

EMBARRASSED—Uncomfortable, uneasy, and nervous.

LOGO—A symbol or design that represents a company or team.

POTENTIAL—The ability to become better.

PRESS CONFERENCE—A meeting in which a person answers questions from reporters.

PREVAILED—Won.

STRATEGY—A plan or method for succeeding.

STUNNED—Shocked and surprised.

SYNTHETIC—Made in a laboratory, not in nature.

Places to Go

ON THE ROAD

NEW JERSEY DEVILS
165 Mulberry Street
Newark, New Jersey 07102
(973) 757-6100

THE HOCKEY HALL OF FAME
Brookfield Place
30 Yonge Street
Toronto, Ontario, Canada   M5E 1X8
(416) 360-7765

ON THE WEB

THE NATIONAL HOCKEY LEAGUE   www.nhl.com
  • *Learn more about the National Hockey League*

THE NEW JERSEY DEVILS   devils.nhl.com
  • *Learn more about the Devils*

THE HOCKEY HALL OF FAME   www.hhof.com
  • *Learn more about hockey's greatest players*

ON THE BOOKSHELF

To learn more about the sport of hockey, look for these books at your library or bookstore:

  • Keltie, Thomas. *Inside Hockey! The Legends, Facts, and Feats that Made the Game.* Toronto, Ontario, Canada: Maple Tree Press, 2008.

  • MacDonald, James. *Hockey Skills: How to Play Like a Pro.* Berkeley Heights, New Jersey: Enslow Elementary, 2009.

  • Stewart, Mark and Kennedy, Mike. *Score! The Action and Artistry of Hockey's Magnificent Moment.* Minneapolis, Minnesota: Lerner Publishing Group, 2010.

Index

PAGE NUMBERS IN **BOLD** REFER TO ILLUSTRATIONS.

The Team

MARK STEWART has written over 200 books for kids—and more than a dozen books on hockey, including a history of the Stanley Cup and an authorized biography of goalie Martin Brodeur. He grew up in New York City during the 1960s rooting for the Rangers and now lives in New Jersey, where he attends Devils games at the Prudential Center. He especially likes the special all-you-can-eat seating section. Mark comes from a family of writers. His grandfather was Sunday Editor of *The New York Times* and his mother was Articles Editor of *Ladies' Home Journal* and *McCall's*, and also wrote for *Sports Illustrated*. Mark has profiled hundreds of athletes over the last 20 years. He has also written several books about New York and New Jersey. Mark is a graduate of Duke University, with a degree in History. He lives with his daughters and wife Sarah overlooking Sandy Hook, New Jersey.

DENIS GIBBONS is a former newsletter editor of the Toronto-based Society for International Hockey Research (SIHR) and a writer and editor with *The Hockey News*. He was a contributing writer to the publication *Kings of the Ice: A History of World Hockey* and has worked as chief hockey researcher at six Winter Olympics for the ABC, CBS, and NBC television networks. Denis also has worked as a researcher for the FOX Sports Network during the Stanley Cup playoffs. He resides in Burlington, Ontario, Canada with his wife Chris.